The Cato Institute

The Cato Institute is named for the libertarian pamphlets, *Cato's Letters,* which were inspired by the Roman Stoic, Cato the Younger. Written by John Trenchard and Thomas Gordon, *Cato's Letters* were widely read in the American colonies in the early eighteenth century and played a major role in laying the philosophical foundation for the revolution that followed.

The erosion of civil and economic liberties in the modern world has occurred in concert with a widening array of social problems. These disturbing developments have resulted from a major failure to examine social problems in terms of the fundamental principles of human dignity, economic welfare, and justice.

The Cato Institute aims to broaden public policy debate by sponsoring programs designed to assist both the scholar and the concerned layperson in analyzing questions of political economy.

The programs of the Cato Institute include the sponsorship and publication of basic research in social philosophy and public policy; publication of major journals on the scholarship of liberty and commentary on political affairs; production of debate forums for radio; and organization of an extensive program of symposia, seminars, and conferences.

CATO INSTITUTE
1700 Montgomery Street
San Francisco, California 94111

Strategic Disengagement and World Peace

Strategic Disengagement and World Peace

Toward a Noninterventionist American Foreign Policy

Earl C. Ravenal

With a Foreword by Felix Morley

CATO PAPER No. 7

CATO
INSTITUTE
San Francisco, California

The first essay in this Cato Paper, "The Case for Strategic Disengagement," is reprinted by permission from *Foreign Affairs,* April 1973. Copyright 1973 ©by Council on Foreign Relations, Inc.

The second essay, "Toward Nuclear Stability," is reprinted from the September 1977 issue of *The Atlantic,* with the permission of the copyright holder, The Atlantic Monthly Company, ©1977.

Both essays have been slightly revised by the author.

ISBN: 0-932790-07-0

Printed in the United States of America.

CATO INSTITUTE
1700 Montgomery Street
San Francisco, California 94111

CONTENTS

Foreword   *Felix Morley*   ix

Part One
The Case for Strategic Disengagement   1

Part Two
Toward Nuclear Stability   23

Recommended Reading   41

About the Author   49

FOREWORD

College catalogs notwithstanding, there is really no such academic discipline as "Political Science." Every professional politician can attest to this. Indeed, it is the complete lack of reliable scientific content that makes "the great game of politics" so generally interesting. Of course, there are public opinion polls, often helpful in arranging bets. But there are no laboratory facilities for testing what will work and what will not. All politics, domestic and (even more so) international, is a gamble—there is no surely predictable outcome.

There is, however, an attainable and valuable procedure known as the scientific approach to politics. At least as old as Aristotle, it has been responsible for most of the progress achieved by mankind in our difficult task of building viable political communities. This scientific approach demands the complete elimination of subjective factors and a detailed knowledge of constitutional anatomy, as thorough as the knowledge of human anatomy exhibited by the surgeon who operates on a cancerous growth. The scientific method has therefore failed most conspicuously in the field of foreign policy, where practitioners can be secretive without possessing expertise and where the voters are generally ill-informed and consequently easily deceived.

The two world wars brought great disillusion to American students of foreign policy because of the failure of collective action by both of the overpromoted international organizations created in the aftermath of each war—the League of Nations and the United Nations. With faith in the latter diminished, it is natural that a new generation of American foreign policy scholars should be active in seeking less hit-or-miss procedures. We are all concerned with this quest, because we are inextricably involved in many international problems and because our diplomatic record in trying to solve them single-handed is dismal and intolerably extravagant.

With any sifting of the work of independent thinkers in the field of foreign policy, the name of Earl C. Ravenal, author of the two papers in the following monograph, comes quickly to the fore. His approach is definitely scientific, distinguished not only by its detachment but equally by restrained objectives. Dr. Ravenal is not composing a Utopian formula but admittedly a "second-best order" wherein the United States may play a respectable part in preventing, rather than provoking, additional world catastrophe. The two articles reproduced herewith are illustrative. That on "The Case for Strategic Disengagement," from *Foreign Affairs* of April 1973, is a blueprint of the author's general design. The supplementary article, "Toward Nuclear Stability," was first printed in *The Atlantic* of September 1977. It applies the underlying thesis to the immediate issue of the pending SALT agreement, negotiated with mutual and retarding mistrust by suspicious executives of the United States and the USSR.

A distinctive feature of Dr. Ravenal's work is his insistence on the fair presentation of viewpoints with which, for good and sufficient reasons, he will ultimately disagree. This is disconcerting, even confusing, for those accustomed to forming opinions at third hand from the casual observations of radio commentators or the emotionally selected evidence of partisans. Because it is never superficial, the Ravenal argument may lose force with those whose thinking is conditioned to superficiality. By the same token it gains with all who have learned that for some problems there are no glib and rose-colored answers. In writing our Constitution, the Founding Fathers did not claim omniscience, but could at least face major issues squarely. One must hope that this capacity has not been altogether lost.

Unlike some political theorists, Dr. Ravenal is thoroughly familiar with the history of his own country. He knows that the United States was established as a federal republic, with separate and divided political powers, not only as among the executive, legislature, and judiciary in the national government, but also as between this central authority and the still partially autonomous constituent states. This system was designed to check, and with weak party discipline will continue to check, adventurism by any President or White House circle. In the field of foreign policy, the latent blockage will be less pronounced if the populace believes itself endangered, or if the President has the rare political dexterity of an FDR. But in such cases an eventual swing back to self-assertion at the grassroots is to be expected. American institutions are for the most part based on local self-government. This precious heritage must always yield to the secretive centralization demanded by an adventurous foreign policy. If the latter produces only successive failures, at prohibitive cost, it is time for responsible husbandry, as Professor Ravenal tells us, to take stock.

Double-digit inflation, unremitting taxation, fuel shortage, and the threat of reimposed conscription—all these are in part due to an overextended foreign policy, and the American people are wondering whether the game is worth its cost. They are not disposed to kowtow to the Kremlin, but neither is it plausible to suppose that the much derided Communist system is about to be enforced on us by marching muzhiks. The clear and present danger is that the limitless demands of "national security" will, not too gradually, erode our freedom from within. The global strategists in Washington must realize that they can easily make "commitments" which the public will be unwilling to support. The lesson of Vietnam is not forgotten.

All this is clearly in Professor Ravenal's mind as he presents "The Case for Strategic Disengagement." The formula cannot properly be called isolationist, since it does not imply withdrawal from any nonmilitary international undertaking. It does mean that secretive and extravagant executive entanglements, often with dictatorial cliques as unpopular as that of the former shah of

Iran, should be abandoned promptly and without apologies. Incidentally, it is noteworthy that disengagement advocates are now numerous among those cosmopolitan Americans who are most familiar with the language, history, and culture of other countries. It is our imperialism that has sponsored "Yankee, go home!"

Those who consider foreign policy a purely executive prerogative are prone to attack the Ravenal thesis as representing a "failure of will." It could perhaps better be called an affirmation of that will for responsible self-government which is the most fundamental and enduring of all our political traditions.

May 1979   Felix Morley

Part One

The Case for Strategic Disengagement

The Case for Strategic Disengagement

Characteristic of American foreign policy since World War II has been the quest for a certain minimum of world order and a practical maximum of American control. Successive schemes for the regulation of power—collective security, bipolar confrontation, and now perhaps the balance of power—have differed in their ob jects and style. But interventionism—structuring the external political-military environment and determining the behavior of other nations, whether in collaboration, conflict, or contention with them—has been the main underlying dimension of our policy. There has been no serious substantive challenge to this premise since the eve of our entry into World War II. The last "great debate," in 1951, over the dispatch of American troops to Europe, was about implementation and constitutional procedure.

How the world might look now had the United States not exercised itself for these thirty years, and how it might look thirty years from now if we were to cease exercising ourselves, are open to conjecture. More certain are the failures of deterrence and the costs of war and readiness. These speculations and reflections are materials for a larger debate about the critical objects and operational style of our foreign policy.

It is time for such a debate. We are at a turning point in our conception of the shape of the international system and our perception of the necessities and responsibilities it imposes on our foreign policy. This is more than the feeling that any year of crisis is a turning point, and more than the hope that after the tunnel of a long and obscure war we must be emerging into a new valley. Rather, longer historical perspective and larger categories of analysis indicate that the second of the major structural systems

3

that followed World War II—bipolar confrontation—has been played out, and a new, but severely limited, set of alternative international systems is pending as both object and determinant of American foreign policy.

These are the alternatives: (1) A limited constellation of powerful nations or blocs, all fully engaged and all with a stake in preserving the system, even at the cost of occasional forcible exercises; differing politically and contending economically, but observing certain "mutual restraints" or rules of engagement—in short, a balance of power. And (2) a more extensive and less-ordered dispersion of nation-states, great, large, and medium in size and "weight," with relative power a less critical factor in assessing and constructing relationships; agnostic about maintaining the shape and tone of the system as a whole, and not bound to restrain other—especially distant—nations for the sake of their own security or the integrity of the system. The latter system has no conventional verbal handle. We might call it "general unalignment," or "a pluralism of unaligned states." It is the baseline condition, the limiting case, of the international system—actually a quasi-anarchy, the situation that is reached if the major nations stop striving to impose external order. This system—or perhaps nonsystem—is the only present alternative to the balance of power (objective conditions not favoring the imposition of universal domination, the achievement of collective security, or the restoration of alliance leadership and bipolar confrontation); and it may well be its historical successor.

This analysis might seem abstract and impractical, were it not for the fact that several successive Administrations have been sensitive to these large-scale alternatives and convinced of the importance of establishing a version of the balance of power. In particular, the Nixon-Kissinger Administration seemed to be aware of the restricted palette of foreign-policy choice, which it characterized prejudicially as "engagement" (the rhetorical concomitant of the balance of power) or "isolationism" (the presumed counterpart of international anarchy). But to describe the choice in such flat terms is to efface the moral dimension of a foreign policy. For example, the balance of power—seen as a policy rather than a system—should be defined not simply by its main dimension of interventionism (or its euphemism, "engagement"), but also by another dimension: that of amoralism.

Similarly, the alternative policy orientation of nonintervention should be defined two-dimensionally: It can be either amoral or moral. Amoral noninterventionism *is* "isolationism." It connotes Fortress America, narrow prejudice, and active xenophobia. It is hard to subscribe to this isolationism; but it may be fair to abstain from its further condemnation, if only because this condemnation has become a mindless litany, and because the diametrically opposite course of national action—moralistic interventionism—has often led beyond the point of general damage to the brink of universal disaster.

The other, moral, style of noninterventionism is not isolationism at all. Rather, it reflects (a) a strict and consistent principle of nonintervention in the political-military order, and (b) a concern for constructive contact with the world. Such a foreign policy orientation might be called "strategic disengagement."

Thus, the balance of power, as system or policy, is neither an inevitable development nor a unique response. The "other" major international system, general unalignment, is a possible world—even a probable world, in time. And the "other" major foreign policy orientation, strategic disengagement, is a viable mode of behavior for the United States, indeed an appropriate mode if the international system continues to evolve toward a more diffused condition.

Unfortunately, the rhetoric of disengagement, unless it is presented meretriciously as a "new internationalism," is not appealing. Particularly in seasons of peace and reconciliation, it may seem ungenerous to project skepticism about the future of world order, and to prescribe the curtailment of international ambition and the pursuit of national immunity. And it is bound to be diminishing for Americans—who are used to hearing that their identity depends on a special responsibility for world order—to be told that they ought to give up their honorable pretensions and to live modestly, like other nations.

But international politics is full of ironies, and not the least of them is that the desire to do good often leads to objective harm. Private virtues are often public vices; national virtues are often international vices. Even the most attractive motives, caring and helping, can be a source of danger and destruction. Conversely, even the private vice of indifference to disorder might, in this imperfect world of fragmented sovereignties, translate into the public virtues of preserving internal integrity and respecting external reality. If we can recognize these ironies of international politics, why should we resist their codification in a coherent scheme of national conduct?

II

Strategic disengagement is both a policy and the end-state of a policy. It can be defined, first, by exclusion—by differentiating it from other positions that are critical or limitationist. It is not the "old isolationism"; it has no xenophobic animus and does not entail autarky. It is not "neoisolationism" or "new isolationism"; these doctrines seem too eclectic in their criteria—sometimes evasively circumstantial, sometimes unabashedly geographical (merely a cover for a Europe-first policy), and sometimes vaguely sentimental. It is not the "new internationalism"; this misleading verbal straddle usually ends in moralistic interventionism, relying half-seriously on the resurrection of a potent United Nations. It is not "benign neglect"—simply because it is neither necessarily benign nor deliberately negligent. It is not just "never again," a narrowly based and intellectually confused reaction to the trauma of Vietnam, which could have only limited instrumental lessons for weapons, tactics, strategy, or military organization. It is not a "spheres of influence" doctrine, either naive or "mature";[1] it implies no collusion in others' spheres and claims none of its own.

Neither is it a "national interest" policy; this perennial realist calculus lends itself as much to the extension as to the limitation of objects of intervention, and can lead, in a sort of perversion, to inconsistent, case-by-case, cost-benefit decisions, on the least-

[1]See Ronald Steel, "A Spheres-of-Influence Policy," *Foreign Policy,* Winter 1971–72.

principled grounds. Nor has it much to do with arbitrary criteria, such as the limitation of troops abroad;[2] this is a technical indicator that may express tactical decision or budgetary restriction, not absence of commitment. And it should go without saying that it is not the equivalent of the Nixon Doctrine, which was a program of force substitution, not substantive disengagement.

Strategic disengagement should also not be implicated with the so-called isolationist personality—a pathological condition combining limited intellect and defective character that is much analyzed in meticulous but misdirected social science. Even if such social-psychologizing correctly identified the clinical syndrome, it would still not settle the policy debate. For one thing, the "behavior" of nations is not equivalent to the aggregate behavior of their citizens, or even the modal behavior of their leaders; the policies of nations are not crude analogues of the intentions of individuals, but are the structured responses of systems to complex goals and complex constraints. And furthermore, whatever else foreign policy may be, it is also strategic, in the sense that it is deliberate, objective, and rational choice, and is determined—and must be judged—more by its consequences than its impulses.

And finally, strategic disengagement is not to be equated with "appeasement." The salient aspect of Munich—apart from the fact that the United States did not even participate—is that the powers that did conceive that short-lived solution *imposed* it on Czechoslovakia in an extension of *active* diplomatic meddling— the very opposite of disengagement. Similarly, the proposal of unilateral withdrawal from Indochina—which was buried by the actual Vietnam settlement—was falsely characterized by its opponents: They likened it to "conniving at the overthrow of our South Vietnamese ally" in order to negotiate our exit from the war. Such a duplicitous course was a highly *conditional* alternative and *would* have constituted appeasement. In absolute contrast, unilateral withdrawal was a completely *unconditional* position—though it would have had extensive implications.

[2]See Michael Roskin, "What 'New Isolationism'?" *Foreign Policy,* Spring 1972.

A second way to define strategic disengagement is by its con-
notations. Its keynote is large-scale adjustment to the international system, rather than detailed control of it. It is a prescription
for an orderly withdrawal from our political-military commitments to other nations and from our military positions
overseas, in a deliberate and measured fashion, with the timetable
determined by our unilateral judgment but responsive to oppor-
tune circumstances and to the sensibilities of our allies and the
conduct of our adversaries. Above all, it would be paced, not
precipitate. To reach the end-state of the disengaged posture
might take one or even two decades of initiatives and diplomacy.

Strategic disengagement comprises two syndromes: The first
centers on the dissolution of alliances and includes rehabilitation
of the civilized concept of neutrality, respect for international law
(even if often its observance is asymmetrical and its sanctions only
symbolic), and relations with any effective government regardless
of its complexion. The second centers on a strict but limited
definition of national security and includes acceptance of revolu-
tionary change in the world, acquiescence even in the forcible
rearrangement of other countries, and adoption of second-chance
military strategies.

A third definition of strategic disengagement is by its geographical extension—where we would draw our security perimeter
on the map. But this should be only illustratively sketched, rather
than rigidly drawn. The reason for this reservation has to do with
the meaning of "policy." Policy is not a set of instant declaratory
propositions; rather, it is the total, but future, orientation of a
system to contingencies, including some now unknown in their
most relevant features. Thus we can talk competently about
general policy orientations, but only tentatively about specific
policy objects.

However, a quick, and thus more than otherwise provocative,
tour of the world would yield these ultimate implications. Asia
might be the earliest theater for the implementation of disengagement. The United States would withdraw to a mid-Pacific position and observe—but not necessarily count on or promote—the
probable emergence of an East Asian regional configuration of

China, Japan, and Russia. We would seek no positions in the Indian Ocean; in South Asia a lesser regional array might emerge, consisting of India, supported by Russia and countered by China and the rump of Pakistan.

In the Middle East, the United States would not attempt to impose a settlement on the contending local states. We would enjoy as long as possible the flow of oil on reasonable commercial terms, and would yield with decent grace and little brandishing of force if seriously challenged by local irresponsibility or outside intervention.

In Western Europe, America would witness the continuing devolution of military power and fragmentation of political will, without making intricate efforts to control NATO or its deployment of forces—aspects that are obviously related. In fact, we would initiate the thinning out of our troops and continue a measured and irreversible redeployment to the continental United States, removing most of the redeployed units from our active structure and dispensing with most of the airlift and sealift and sea-control forces that are justified solely for reinforcement and resupply in an extended ground war in Europe.

III

Why do it? Why adopt a policy of strategic disengagement? In doing anything, one either initiates, hoping to achieve some gain or improvement, or responds, adjusting to a situation. Strategic disengagement has elements of both, but more of the latter. It is an anticipatory adjustment—a long, major adaptation to an evolutionary process in the international system and a basic social situation in the United States.

Nevertheless, there are some benefits, though these are not so much reasons for doing it as reasons for being glad to have done it. First, this posture does have tangible consequences for defense preparations—force structures, weapons systems, and budgets. Though cost saving might not be the main determinant of this policy, it is not a contemptible byproduct. In fact, the only way honestly to achieve meaningful defense budget cuts—of the

9

magnitude mentioned in the 1972 presidential campaign (but not since then), on the order of $35 billion a year—is to execute a far-reaching program of strategic disengagement.

Another positive reason for strategic disengagement is to avoid the possible moral "costs" of conflict. These costs are not negligible and impose their own constraints in the form of international diplomatic reactions and domestic social pressures, which might limit our ability to persevere in a conflict. Moral costs can attach either to indecisive conflicts protracted by self-limitation or, conversely, to decisive measures to end conflict.

But the principal reason for strategic disengagement is to make an adjustment that will have sufficient coherence to weather a future of perplexing variations in the pressure of circumstances and the incidence of accidental events.

What, then, is this expected future to which we are adjusting? We can identify six critical conditions in the future international system: The first is the high probability of troubles, such as embargoes, expropriations, coups, revolutions, externally supported subversions, thrusts by impatient irredentist states, and calculated probes of defense perimeters. These will be neither resolved nor constructively equilibrated by some benign balance-of-power mechanism. All of these situations could have consequences that would be unfavorable to U.S. interests. But they would threaten the central security of the United States only to the extent that we "adopted" them in ways that made them security issues, through such instruments as alliances, guarantees, collective security arrangements, and unilateral commitments by declaration or implicit orientation. In that case, any of these situations could begin an escalatory antiphony of deterrent threats, challenges, and credibility-maintaining countermoves.

The second tendency is increasing interdependence—but this has a different implication from the one which proponents of interdependence recognize. Interdependence, in these terms, is a set of functional linkages of nations: resources—raw materials, energy and food; access routes—commercial and strategic; economic activities—trade, monetary and investment, and their patterns and organizations; populations—with their movements and impacts; and the physical environment. These areas harbor problems that could be aggravated to the point where they became threats to the security of nations, demanding, not suggesting, solutions.

The third element of the future international system is the probable absence of an ultimate adjustment mechanism in the form of a supranational institution that can authoritatively dispense justice and grant relief, especially in those extreme cases that threaten to unhinge the system—though in lesser cases of international disorder, mediation and peacekeeping might be effective, and in other functional areas some organized cooperation will exist. Even the tacit "rules" of the balance of power will break down precisely when they are most needed. These rules are not positive restraints, or even reliable predictions of the behavior of nations in the pursuit of their interests, but, rather, mere system-maintenance conditions—descriptions of ideal conduct that derive from the very definition of a balance of power.

The fourth factor is an interim conclusion of the first three—that stabilization, the long-range action of states to bring about conditions in the external system that enhance their security, will take the form of unilateral intervention rather than collaborative world order.

The fifth future condition is the unmanageable diffusion of power beyond some ideal geometry of powerful but responsible states. Instead, this process is likely to proceed to a kaleidoscopic interaction of multiple political entities. By any measure of power—military (nuclear or conventional, actual or potential), economic (total wealth or commercial weight), or political (the will to autonomy and achievement)—there may be fifteen or twenty salient states, not necessarily equal and not necessarily armed with nuclear weapons, but potent to the point of enjoying the possibility of independent action. This would be a "Gaullist world."

The diffusion of power will have several aspects: One is that limits will become evident in existing unions, and cracks will appear in existing military alliances. Europe, for example, may agglomerate further, but it will not integrate politically. The Atlantic Alliance also will suffer from a continuing divergence of interests and allegiances. There will be the traditional cultural tug of Europe as an entity, and the blandishment of commercial deals with Eastern Europe, reinforcing the desire of individual allies for political maneuverability and military autonomy. Allies will increasingly, despite occasional contributions toward specific infrastructural items, fail to bear their "fair share" of the burdens of the Alliance and will demand a disproportionate share—or, bad enough, a proportionate share—of command authority. And there will be, within the Atlantic Alliance (and our Asian alliances as well), dissonance over the suitability of foreign policies, strategies, and weapons systems. The result is that alliances and multinational groupings will become the least-efficient instruments for bargaining among the principal antagonists in the international system. Individual nations are already seeking out their adversaries directly, in order to make general political arrangements and specific deals on economic, environmental, and resource issues.

Another aspect of diffusion is the impracticality of military power, whether nuclear, conventional, or subconventional. Nuclear force, used or threatened, could be a trigger to uncontrollable or unpredictable violence, immediately or in the longer run because of adverse precedents. Conventional military power is increasingly ineffective in relative terms, because of the rising cost of its application and the diminishing value of its effects in politically unfocused, or geographically intractable, or great-power-stalemated situations. And subconventional force is vitiated by its unreliable byproducts: It creates embarrassing clients, diminishes diplomatic maneuverability, and invites escalation once a minimal stake is established.

The sixth condition that will complicate the enforcement of international order is the lack of consensus in domestic support—not when our system is free from external pressure, but precisely when it most needs steady support. Few societies—especially one such as the United States—will hold together in foreign exercises that are ill-defined or, conversely, dedicated to the maintenance of a balance of power. Indeed, the

12

Nixon-Kissinger Administration did not cultivate active, fervent public support. Acquiescence was entirely sufficient, and more appropriate, for a subtle, flexible balance-of-power policy—as long as it was limited to the faint demonstration of force. But where escalation was required to validate an earlier countermeasure that was indecisive, support proved to be lacking and intervention failed before it had achieved its effect. The lack of public support might not prevent intervention, but it might critically inhibit its prosecution.

Let us return for a moment to draw some conclusions about interdependence. The typical argument for interdependence recites the material or spiritual facts that *push* and *throw* nations together and concludes with the "ethical necessity" of binding nations together in world order. It urgently, humanely, reminds us that we are living in One World. But it fails to recognize a paradox that is embedded in the situation:

1. Interdependence creates the need for more world order—the authority to restrain and dispose— without creating order itself. Indeed, it diminishes the effectiveness of the existing degree of world order, which might be barely viable only because it is relatively unstressed. In short, interdependence, which is widely mistaken for part of the solution, is actually part of the problem.

2. The diffusion of power—in the form of the persistence and increasing authority of the nation-state, and the increasing impotence of constructive coercion—prevents the more perfect world order required by the conditions of interdependence.

3. But, paradoxically, both interdependence and diffusion are simultaneously increasing in the world. And since diffusion causes disorder, while interdependence merely requires order, the prognosis is more disorder in the international system.

Now, if the foreign policy of an individual state could be logically ideal, it would either cut down on interdependence in order to be freer from the uncontrollable effects of the system, or would reverse the diffusion of power by gaining more control over the system. But neither of these logically ideal courses is within the scope of a single nation's policy. Interdependencies cannot be avoided at will, since they are primarily created not by

13

the policy of the nation but by factors that are outside the frame of choice at the national level. And, conversely, the attempt to increase or manipulate power—even constructively—would be resisted by jealous and defensive nation-states.

So nations will have to live with greater interdependence, but in the face of less world order. Thus, a general policy prescription, confronting these contradictory tendencies, would have to be formulated in a "split level."

The face of the policy would be hopeful and constructive, selectively accommodating interdependence—stressing practical cooperation in specific areas, encouraging the universal observance of an international law of self-restraint, and joining in the mediation of disputes and some limited but noncommittal peacekeeping.

But the residual level of the policy would be skeptical and defensive, hedging and insulating against disorder. Where other nations could expropriate our investments or interdict our access to raw materials or energy resources, we would hedge—the only alternatives being deprivation or gunboat diplomacy. And where trading patterns might become adverse, we would adjust our expectations toward import substitution; this does not imply instant autarky, but gearing the mind and the system to deal with incipient mercantilism by means other than irrelevant bluster. This policy also favors an international monetary system that depends on the implicit flexibility of exchange rates, rather than the necessity of explicit initiatives and bargaining.

In political-military arrangements, we would insulate. Security frontiers would be retracted to defensible lines that corresponded generally to national boundaries and related ocean areas. Force structures and base locations would change accordingly. Military strategies would not be absolutely frozen, but would be capable of second-chance reactions, in case major calculations were upset by events or impending events. Strategic nuclear sufficiency would be maintained. But commitments would be gradually dissolved. We might hope that affected nations would adopt compensatory measures that were sensible and stable, but there would be little way to enforce our preferences. And we would not contribute to

14

their compensatory measures to the point where we were recommitted.

IV

Is strategic disengagement feasible for the United States? Part of the answer lies in the way the question is posed. It is often posed in a falsely static form: Can the United States even think of opting out of the international system, *as it is?* And in circumstances that seem to be a dereliction of responsibility or a breach of the rules of the system?

Rather, the question should be put in dynamic form: Can the United States adjust to the system *as it would be changed* by its own behavior? For one quality of a great power is that its major choices define the structure of the international system, not simply influence its process.

Of course, the malleability of the international system is not unlimited. By its defection, a great power can defeat any existent scheme of world order; but it cannot necessarily create new ones by its own intention and means. Thus, in present circumstances, single-nation hegemony is obviously an impossibility. And various forms of collective security, including a condominium of superpowers, seem beyond attainment. The bipolar order is passing and defies restoration, though certain of its features persist—notably, the formal alliances and the habits of zero-sum strategic thinking. But recalcitrant allies, third forces, and cross-cutting institutions are too prevalent. So there remain the practical alternatives of a multipolar balance of power or a pluralism of unaligned states.

We are asking, then, whether the United States can live in a situation of general unalignment which its own conduct would materially help to establish. This question has its tangible and its intangible components.

The tangible questions are: Would such a situation be minimally supportive of the political and economic life of the state? Can the nation live with the consequences of its failure to intervene readily with sufficient force to preserve its real interests, principally its access as a key to further benefits from the external system? Can it even defend what it must unavoidably defend—its own existence and integrity—if it allows certain ancillary strategic assets to go by the board? Can it credibly deter the central threats to its existence if it declines to deter lesser threats to lesser objects? To what extent is it implicitly dependent on the self-restraint of other nations, or the simple hope that they will fail in the attainment of their objectives?

The intangible questions are: Could our system adjust to the probable "loss" of some previously valued objects—no less real, though intangible and indirect in their impact on our security—the slippage of allegiances, the lapse of comfortable relationships, the extension of hostile control? The adjustment to intangible loss may be the most critical condition for the viability of a policy of strategic disengagement.

A posture of strategic disengagement is favored by several factors, some peculiar to the American situation and some generic. The first is a condition which we have mentioned in another context as a *reason* for disengagement: the increasing diffusion of usable power among nations. This is not the same as an assertion of "no threat." It is to say that the same condition that frustrates the exercise of American control also frustrates the efforts of competitive states to profit directly and proportionally from our withdrawal, and would mitigate the consequences for us even if they were to succeed.

The second factor has impressed observers as a reason, and a condition, for disengagement since the time of George Washington: the peculiar geographic position of the United States ("Our detached and distant situation invites us to a different course and enables us to pursue it. . . ."). Even—perhaps especially—in the nuclear age, geography still confers military advantage and allows political-military detachment,[3] as long as it is

---

[3]A contrary case is made by Albert Wohlstetter ("Illusions of Distance," *Foreign Affairs,* January 1968) on the basis of logistical and technological factors, which overcome raw distance. But logistics and technology are not the whole point, nor is raw distance, without the help of other dimensions of geography. Every tactical commander realizes the obstructive value of an earthwork, or a fifty-yard ditch

complemented by a third factor—adequate conventional military forces.

A fourth factor that permits a disengaged political-military stance is nuclear weapons. This factor has two dimensions. On the one hand, for the individual nation, nuclear weapons are like certain other military and situational resources writ large. For example, a secure nuclear retaliatory capability is, for the United States in the twentieth century, the equivalent of the protection of the British fleet in the halcyon era of American isolation, the nineteenth century.

On the other hand, for the international system, nuclear weapons have extraordinary consequences. The distribution of nuclear force ushers in a distinctive variant of the international system of general unalignment—a "veto" system, in which the competent nations pursue independent foreign policies and protect their autonomy with the power to maim an attacker. Even threshold nuclear powers, such as Japan, partake indirectly of this quality, just as analogously in a balance-of-power system nations can wield power by allying and threatening, though limited war is the residual arbiter of that system.

In fact, nuclear weapons precipitate a gradual and inexorable movement toward unalignment—beyond a balance of power—once they are held by more than one potential major antagonist. It is wrong to attribute this effect to the general proliferation of nuclear weapons among third, fourth, or fifth states, including lesser alliance partners. The point of no return occurs when two "polar" powers have attained them. The rest is an inevitable disintegration and an eventual transformation—the logical progression to a "Gaullist world."

The French did not create this condition; nor did they merely react to it. They anticipated it, even before de Gaulle's return to

---

such as the Suez Canal. A fortiori, the Pacific Ocean remains a formidable barrier, cheap for transport no doubt, but forbidding for conventional invasion. (Central nuclear protection, of course, is a separate problem and a discontinuous calculus.) Barriers force the enemy to stop and mass, and—perhaps most important—put upon him the onus of unmistakable initiative. We are reminded again that arguments deriving from a "shrinking world" must always be qualified.

power in 1958, and began to draw the correct (though not the only possible) policy conclusions, however unpalatable these might have been for the United States. The standard American characterizations of national nuclear forces as completely useless because militarily useless, and at best (or at worst) a "trigger" for the American deterrent, are wide of the mark. A national nuclear force might not be much "good" in a strict military calculus of reciprocal destruction. But this is not the intention of its architects. Its purpose is political—not in the trivial sense of an entrance ticket to a prestigious "club," but in the most profound sense of that term.[4]

For a medium power, such as France, the utility of nuclear weapons lies not in any plausible coercive strategy, but only in a desperate retaliation, defensive in strategic significance even though "offensive" in military form. Thus the contemplated use of nuclear weapons by a people will be credible if, and only if, it is in the "final defense of their supreme self-interest." And conversely, in that extreme context, any other protection—through generalized "umbrellas," multilateral nonproliferation treaties, or the calculated interest of alliance partners—will not be credible or, to the ultimately logical nuclear theorist, even necessary.

For the nuclear superpower, the potency of its own weapons, and their limitations in the face of other nations' weapons, will have two effects that reinforce each other. First, it will *not need* to acknowledge a seamless web of degrees and cases of deterrence; it can be content to default on nonvital foreign commitments. And second, it may be *deterred* from fulfilling purely external commitments; regardless of their merit, it will be pressed to default on them by the risk to its own central security. Thus a veto system allows, but also demands, tolerance of very wide swings of accumulated power before any counteraction is indicated (though it is also difficult to see how any other power would risk the aggressive moves necessary to accumulate such power).

For these reasons, nuclear weapons, once beyond the posses-

---

[4]This is a cardinal concept of the Gaullist nuclear theorists. See, for example, Michel Debré, "France's Global Strategy," *Foreign Affairs,* April 1971.

sion of a single polar power, begin to corrode alliances. No ally can be confident that, in a crisis, it will not be disowned by a joint or senior nuclear protector. Thus, in a veto system, an alliance, to be effective, must approach the status of a political union or a feudal subordination. However, once it has acquired its own nuclear force, there is no particular reason for an ally to pool it within the alliance. The sheer power of the pooled force will probably be redundant; and yet no ally will take advantage of this to cut its force and consent to cost-effective joint targeting if this means delegating to an alien political will—and thus an implicitly untrustworthy ally—the decision to withhold or fire against some vital target. Therefore, nuclear weapons ultimately discourage casual and ambiguous commitments and enforce a more severe choice: to create a political community—through union or subordination—integral enough to make mutual nuclear defense credible, or to acquiesce in the dissolution of alliances.

V

Disengagement has been proposed before. It is a perennial response to the insoluble problems of the international system epitomized by periodic wars. It was adopted after World War I, debated after World War II, and advanced in the 1950s as a way out of the cold war. It is an authentic vision—not necessarily noble, but often practical and even moral in its tendency to avoid the senseless, unfairly apportioned, and ruinous costs of war.

But somehow the vision is always rejected—sometimes when proposed, sometimes later when our national response is tested. The nation, and even some of the proponents of disengagement respond to strategic challenge with reengagement, intervention, and war. What goes wrong? Possibly this: (1) In prospect, disengagement seems too comprehensive, too extreme; it seems to involve us in an undifferentiated retreat from the world, a kind of total—even amoral—isolationism. And (2) in the moment of truth, when an issue threatens to become strategic, in scale and in political-military effect, we are not willing to lose—that is, to risk the consequences of nonintervention.

For the critical question in any proposal of disengagement is not its techniques and provisions, but rather our strategic concern for the objects at risk in the proposal. As long as we maintain this strategic concern, any scheme of disengagement will be vulnerable to objection on its own terms: It cannot ensure that we will not "lose" and our adversaries will not "gain."

It was really on this point that George Kennan's scheme of disengagement in Central Europe in the late 1950s foundered. He argued for the avoidance of risk and tension, the extension of incentive and reassurance to the Soviets, the futility of defense through NATO, and the greater chance of healing the division of Europe. The problem was that disengagement was represented as a *better* tactic to advance the interest of the United States in the wholeness, health, and safety of Europe. And for this it required a reciprocal move by our adversary, Russia. Thus, its opponents could demonstrate generally that the risks of this initiative were greater than the possible gains—always in terms of the conceded interest in the condition of Europe—and specifically that the risk of nonadherence by the Soviets to the reciprocal terms was too great and was irreducible. So Kennan's initiative evoked the critical antagonism of Henry Kissinger[5] and the patrician disgust of Dean Acheson.[6] And there is some justice in their reactions. For it is not a valid disengagement if we simply withdraw and continue to hope for the best.

How might a fresh proposal effectively differ? Strategic disengagement depends on the ability, in logic and in fact, to maintain two distinctions. The first is the separation of strategic interests from other concerns, and the sympathetic pursuit of those other nonstrategic concerns in collaborative international bodies and in our own unilateral acts; disengagement should not affect commercial relations, humanitarian expressions, or cultural contacts.

The second is the distinction of objective from nonobjective

[5]"Missiles and the Western Alliance," *Foreign Affairs,* April 1958.
[6]"The Illusion of Disengagement," *Foreign Affairs,* April 1958.

factors. The key to this is the concept of equanimity (or "indifference"). This is *not* an attitude of negligence or unconcern or rejection; it is an acceptance of situations and consequences.

This equanimity is "objective" in several senses of the word: (1) It refers to an *objective* policy orientation, not a subjective psychological state; (2) It is directed to the *objects* of our policy—whether they be the international system as a whole, or particular allied nations, threatened resources, or strategic situations—not the style of our policy-making or its specific values. And in the last resort, it is not even our sympathy for these objects of our policy, or our formal "commitments" to them, but what we consider their strategic *necessity* that implicates us in foreign conflict and virtually dictates our intervention.

Thus, if we are to achieve disengagement, we must make our policy deliberately neutral toward a wide range of differential strategic conditions and outcomes in the world. We will be able to afford this orientation only if we hedge and insulate. But even these are not enough. To sustain a strict and consistent disengagement, our decision-making system must adjust its most fundamental presumptions—about the relevance of threats, the calculus of risks, and the nature of the national interest. These are the primal categories that mold our response to strategic challenge, despite apparent shifts in surface values.

Nevertheless, in final ethical terms, we are left with an unsatisfactory choice: whether to choose the sins of commission and intervention, or the sins of omission and disengagement. We may have to resolve this dilemma on the basis of the Kantian categorical imperative: We cannot control the behavior of others; we can only behave as we will others to behave—though we expect little reciprocity or symmetry. Admittedly, this is not a self-executing policy. But, at least in moral theory, it could be a self-fulfilling prophecy.

21

Part Two

Toward Nuclear Stability

Toward Nuclear Stability *

The Retreat from Moscow

As we approached the expiration of the current SALT (Strategic Arms Limitation Talks) arrangement in October 1977, the only things that were clear were that any agreement achieved would not satisfy the hawks in the Senate, and that it would not remotely resemble Carter's bold "Moscow comprehensive proposal" of the previous spring, which so animated American public opinion and so annoyed the Russians. Why that is so, and what we ought to do about it, are matters of the highest importance. Unfortunately, most comments on the SALT negotiations have been concerned with bureaucratic bargaining, gossip, and mechanics, and have neglected the logic behind the moves.

Why has SALT, up to this point, failed to control the arms race? What are the factors that still threaten the nuclear balance? And how can we extricate ourselves from the growing strategic danger that looms, according to hawks and doves alike, in the future?

To pursue those questions, it is necessary to understand why the Carter Administration put forward its comprehensive arms limitation proposal in Moscow in March 1977. Why, specifically,

---

*This essay is adapted from an article originally written from the perspective of late spring 1977 and published in the September 1977 issue of *The Atlantic*. Since it was not a journalistic report, but rather was designed to frame the logic of the strategic nuclear balance and to propose a policy that would honor the dictates of morality as well as respect the requisites of strategy, for this republication in mid-1979 I have not revised it much. I believe it remains an appropriate analysis of nuclear arms during the SALT II debate, and will remain a valid prescription in the aftermath of the debate.

did it contradict the understandings that were arrived at by Ford and Brezhnev in Vladivostok in November 1974?

What was wrong with the Vladivostok agreement is precisely what the Carter negotiators were trying to remedy in Moscow:

1. The Vladivostok agreement set a ceiling of 2,400 on each side's strategic nuclear delivery vehicles (land-based missiles, sea-based missiles, and bombers), and of 1,320 on those vehicles that are "MIRVed" (that is, carry several independently targetable warheads). Those ceilings were high enough to encompass all the actual forces or the planned buildups of both sides.

2. The agreement set no limit on "throw weight" (a factor which translates roughly into the explosive power that missiles can carry).

Almost no one on the American side—except Kissinger and Ford—really liked the Vladivostok agreement. Both the hawks and the doves, for quite different reasons, would have preferred lower ceilings. The hawks wanted to force the Soviets to dismantle many of their large, heavy missiles. They complained that Vladivostok simply ratified Soviet "superiority"—in total throw weight, total megatonnage, and numbers of delivery vehicles— and that the Soviets would some day *use* this advantage to neutralize our power and force political changes or gain military successes in some important region. How would they do this? Well, according to the "Nitze scenario,"[1] the adversary could threaten a first strike against our land-based missiles and some of our other nuclear forces, reserving enough spare throw weight to hold our cities hostage and deter our retaliatory strike. Nitze called that "deterring our deterrent."

The doves, on the other hand, have never been worried about Soviet "superiority." They wanted ceilings low enough to cause *us* to stop building and upgrading our missiles. They complained about all the additional "overkill" that would be built into the arsenals of both sides.

Both the hawks and the doves are hung up on numbers. But it is

[1]Paul H. Nitze, "Assuring Strategic Stability in an Era of Détente," *Foreign Affairs,* January 1976, and "Deterring Our Deterrent," *Foreign Policy,* Winter 1976–77.

not the numbers that matter. Vladivostok was faulty because it would still allow critical *instabilities* to endanger the strategic balance. Within the Vladivostok limits—the unlimited throw weight, the large MIRV-carrying capacity, the increasing accuracy—either side could destroy or threaten to destroy, in a first strike, a large percentage of the nuclear forces of the other, particularly the other's land-based missiles. You don't have to be a hawk to get the logical bite of that: A significant segment of our "triad" of nuclear forces is becoming technologically vulnerable. Once again, as in the late 1950s, the "balance of terror" is becoming "delicate." Strategic stability could be unhinged.

That is why the Carter Administration was looking for "deep cuts"—particularly cuts that would neutralize the Soviets' capacity to strike at our nuclear forces. (The two critical planks in the Carter proposal at Moscow were [1] the limit on "heavy" missiles, causing the Soviets to reduce their 308 SS-9s and SS-18s to 150, and [2] the limit on land-based MIRVed missiles, 550, which happens by coincidence to be the precise number of *our* land-based MIRVed missiles.) The Administration was looking to SALT—to the formal arms control process—for a solution to our strategic problems.

In fact, a SALT proposal that would significantly lower the overall ceilings on strategic weapons on both sides (but actually pin the Russians down harder) was the *only* way to get the hawks and the doves—the arms expansionists and the arms controllers—together. And it was the last chance, as we are now seeing, before the hawks turned up the heat under a pot of new, potent, sophisticated weapons systems: the MX (the mobile intercontinental ballistic missile); the B-1 bomber; the Trident II longer-range missile and the large submarine that carries it; and the cruise missile, launched from the air, the sea, or the land.

Thus even more portentous than the Moscow initiative and failure was Carter's subsequent press conference, in which he said he "would be forced to" step up the development and deployment of these weapons systems if he couldn't get a satisfactory SALT agreement with the Russians.

Some of these weapons systems are frightfully destabilizing   27 (long-range land- or sea-based cruise missiles, and the high yield plus superaccuracy of the MX). Some are "merely" redundant and terribly expensive (the B-1; that is one reason that President Carter halted its production[2]). Some are premature (the Trident II system). And some may even be useful (medium-range air-launched cruise missiles). But worse than the weapons systems are some of the tactics that are emerging again in the face of the Soviet technical threat to our missiles: hair-trigger variants of "launch-on-warning." Call them what you will, even if they provide for disarming missiles in flight, they are awesomely risky and provocative.

The MX itself is a formidable system. It can be mobile or multiply based and it will carry up to fourteen powerful MIRV warheads, each with a yield of about 200 kilotons, equipped with advanced NAVSTAR celestial guidance and MARV terminal guidance for pinpoint accuracy. With such accuracy, we could finally realize Barry Goldwater's vision of "lobbing a nuke right into the men's room of the Kremlin." That kind of accuracy, combined with silo-busting yields, would make the MX a highly unnerving first-strike "counterforce" weapon.

Carter's arms reduction proposal (which would have banned land-mobile systems, the ones the Russians have already deployed and the ones we are developing) stemmed from the Administration's genuine reluctance to deploy the MX, which, among its other liabilities, would cost from $30 to $50 billion. But no one, not even the hawks, prefers to build these weapons systems—*if* we can get the same strategic results by officially disarming the Russians through SALT. That, as the song says, is nice work if you can get it.

There is nothing wrong with using the arms control process to achieve our strategic objectives. The trouble is that the only proposal that would both solve our strategic problems and gain the united support of hawks and doves won't work. The Russians

---

[2]Ironically, Carter's decision to halt the B-1 made it harder to deny the Air Force its advanced land-based missile—and this will be not just expensive but destabilizing.

won't buy it. (Conversely, the only settlement we have been able to get won't solve our strategic problems.) Even Kissinger, with his pursuit of détente and political laissez-faire, knew he couldn't get such an ambitious arms limitation agreement from the Russians. So he didn't even try. How could the Carter Administration, with its intrusive human rights policy, get the Russians to shed their nuclear weaponry?

The End of Arms Control?

The March 1977 proposal at Moscow, of course, was not the end of the road for arms control. The Administration managed to get itself together, approached the Soviets more circumspectly, and resumed discussions at Geneva. And in late July the President sought to mollify the Russians by suggesting that his comprehensive proposal represented only "long-term goals." A SALT II agreement eventually emerged at the Vienna summit in June 1979.

But Moscow did portend something: Future SALT negotiations with the Russians, even if "successful," will fall short of solving our strategic problems. They are unlikely to reduce the number of the Russians' heavy silo-busting missiles below some critical threshold, or curtail their testing of MIRVs or accurate reentry vehicles. In short, the formal arms control process will not eradicate the threat to our land-based missiles and thus cure the instability of the strategic balance.

I don't want to be misunderstood. We *should* continue our negotiations with the Soviets, and aim at genuine agreements. But we have come to expect too much from formal arms control. We have invested SALT—the process, our proposals, even the choice of a chief negotiator—with an inordinate degree of critical importance.

In fact, formal "arms control" implies certain specific conditions: an explicit and semipublic bargaining forum; agreements that carry the expectation of effective inspection and policing; and, above all, reciprocity. (It also gives rise to posturing, stonewalling, constructing bargaining chips, and playing games of "chicken.") It is precisely these conditions that have made it hard

29

to achieve progress in the regulation of arms competition, and, even where agreements have been reached, have given rise to recriminations and accusations of cheating.

What that means is that it is wrong—and even dangerous—to equate "arms control" with the control of arms in the generic sense, let alone with disarmament. What is the point of arms control? Certainly not to attain treaties for their own sake. The objectives of arms control are to stabilize the overall strategic balance; to maintain adequate deterrence; and, possibly, to limit damage to ourselves, and conceivably to others, in the event of a nuclear conflict or accident.

These objectives can still be sought, but not necessarily within the context of formal arms control. We may have to hedge against our inability to achieve them in this or that round of bargaining. We may need to initiate some *unilateral* moves as a backstop to SALT.

The Logic of Incentives

Whether or not these unilateral moves will work depends on the "logic of incentives." Both sides—hawks and doves—are so busy playing the nuclear numbers game that they forget one essential fact: A nuclear war has to be started by someone. So the question is, Why would either side want to strike first?

Is it true that the Russians, the moment they reach some magic number—some critical ratio of "superiority" (either initially, or after projecting the results of a hypothetical nuclear exchange)—will have an incentive to attack? Would they try to cash in their paper superiority, to convert it into the harder coinage of "military victory," by waging a sudden first strike against our nuclear forces? Some of the hawks seem to be saying that. Here is Paul Nitze's statement in "Deterring Our Deterrent": "The [strategic] relationship is becoming unstable [because] the Soviets in coming years will be able to increase their ratio of advantage by attacking U.S. forces."

As if that were all the Russians had to think about. If the Russians are rational (and we must believe—and pray—that they are), *this* is the calculation they must make: They must weigh the prob-

30

able destruction to themselves—their society[3] and their military forces—against the positive value of any political or strategic or economic *gains* to themselves through war. And "gains" do *not* include any pleasure they might take in destroying the United States, or in declaring themselves the winner of a nuclear war. (Moreover, in a world shared by six or seven other nuclear powers—notably China—the Soviets would hardly wish to become a nuclear pygmy by expending their own missiles in an exchange with the United States.)

The doves, too, somehow believe that numbers themselves can lead to nuclear war. Every other day, it seems, you get a piece of second-class mail from these Cassandras of "overkill" saying, ". . . the Pentagon now has the equivalent of 600,000 Hiroshima bombs. . . . We have enough missiles to destroy Russia forty-four times. . . . 20 percent more nuclear weapons deployed than are necessary to destroy the entire human race . . .," etc., etc. The irony is that the doves can talk about overkill precisely because their preferred strategic response is full-scale retaliation, as pure and horrifying as John Foster Dulles ever threatened. All we "need" to execute this kind of strike is a relative handful of megatons left somewhere in our force structure; the rest, by definition, is overkill.

It's easy to see what the doves are driving at—limiting the expansion of nuclear forces, reducing arms costs, and stabilizing the strategic balance without having to match the Russians in every detail. But they aren't improving the public debate. In fact, they are begging the real questions: Overkill *for what?* What are the *targets?* Who would strike first? For what reason? In other

---

[3]This, of course, is where civil defense comes in. There is no doubt that the Russians are spending many times what we do to evacuate and protect urban populations in the event of warning of nuclear war. The full extent of their motives is not clear. The effectiveness of even the most heroic and technically virtuose measures would be vitiated by their severe climate and by the fact that they might have no cities to return to—*if* we pursued a countercity strategy. In sum, it is doubtful that they could escape enough destruction to change their calculation from bad to acceptable. In any case, Russian persistence in civil defense can only support the proposal, offered here, that the United States move to a countermilitary, rather than a countercity, strategy.

words, the numbers don't prove anything. For some strategies we already have twenty times too many warheads or megatons; for others we will never have enough. And getting rid of "surplus" killing power would not in itself improve strategic stability. It all gets back to the strategies themselves. They might be good or bad, but the matter is not self-evident.

So we can dispose of the notion that a nuclear war would start "out of the blue." That's not how it works. A future nuclear war might grow out of some festering, escalating crisis—another confrontation in the Middle East, or a succession dispute in Yugoslavia—where conflict had already been joined and each side had already developed reasons to be nervous about the other's resort to nuclear weapons. *Then,* in this game theorist's nightmare, an edgy or desperate enemy might be inspired to unleash a nuclear strike—*if* he had the technical ability to destroy a large portion of his adversary's nuclear forces.

By the same token, we can dispose of the notion that a nuclear war would start with an attack on cities. There is absolutely no sense in this. A nuclear aggressor would start a war by attempting to disarm as much of his opponent's nuclear force as possible, in order to limit damage to himself from a retaliatory strike.

So, whether we like it or not, we are back to thinking about "counterforce." And the game of counterforce is about the relationship between "their" capability and "our" vulnerability. It can be expressed this way: "They" are capable to the extent that their nuclear force has accuracy and large numbers of warheads. "We" are vulnerable to the extent that our forces are fixed in known places ("sitting ducks") and not well protected (not in hardened shelters and not guarded by antiballistic missiles). A simpler way of summarizing it is this: If they can't disarm us, they aren't going to try to hit us.

A Modest Proposal

The solution to strategic nuclear vulnerability, therefore, may lie not in the expansion of force, as the hawks urge, but in retrenchment, moves of unilateral *restraint*. Previous proposals of unilateral restraint have been viewed as mere gambits, psychological bait, to be withdrawn or reversed if they are not reciprocated. Genuine unilateral moves would have to make strategic sense in themselves, so that they could be sustained whether or not they were reciprocated by the other nuclear superpower.

We can restore strategic stability with a posture that calls for a smaller and cheaper nuclear arsenal, sufficient for purposes of deterrence. To achieve this posture, the United States would abandon all fixed land-based missiles as they become vulnerable to enemy attack, and refrain from replacing them with mobile land-based missiles. (This posture would be accompanied by two changes in nuclear doctrine: noncivilian targeting and no-first-use.) The abandonment of land-based missiles would move the United States away from the present triad of nuclear forces to a dyad consisting of submarines and bombers. We would not make this move hastily, but only as we developed the technology to ensure accurate coverage of equivalent targets with our undersea weapons systems. Among other things, we would need to solve the "command-and-control" problem—the problem of sending foolproof orders and receiving timely information from submarines on station.

There are other things we could do. We could deploy the longer-range Trident I (or C-4) missile, at first installing it in our present Poseidon submarines. This would allow our submarines to operate farther from their targets, closer to their bases, and in a greater area of ocean, extending their invulnerability by complicating the enemy's antisubmarine warfare. We could complement this move by developing medium-range air-launched cruise missiles for our existing B-52 bombers. This is the course President Carter chose in making his decision to dispense with the construction of more B-1 bombers (which would have cost $102 million for each plane).

None of these programs is expansive. Accuracy and command-and-control for sea-based weapons are, for better or worse, already in advanced stages of development. The Trident I missile should be ready for deployment in 1980. The air-launched cruise missile, already far along, is a weapons system that is likely to survive any future SALT restrictions. In fact, the strategic stance outlined here would allow significant savings in the defense budget. Moving to a dyad of forces, and eliminating unneeded air defense, would eventually reduce the cost of strategic forces from the $25 billion requested for fiscal year 1979 to about $18 billion a year (in 1979 dollars).

This position admittedly presents some problems for arms control as it has been conventionally construed. Cruise missiles, in particular, complicate the task of verification (though they don't completely defeat the possibility of controls). But verification is not an independent objective of arms control; it is only a tool. The question is whether we want the semblance of "arms control" or the reality of strategic stability.

Ironically, strategic stability would also be enhanced if the *Russians* shifted from fixed land-based missiles to land-mobile missiles. They would be accomplishing the analogy of our "putting missiles to sea" by using their expansive land mass to conceal their mobile missiles. This, again, would complicate the verification of numbers. But it would also diminish the Soviets' fear of an American first strike.

The move from triad to dyad is *not* a form of "unilateral disarmament." In fact, the United States would gain, not lose. The new posture would enhance strategic stability by reducing incentives for an adversary to strike at our nuclear force. In the peculiar algebra of nuclear strategy, less can be more.

The Moral Dimension

Now, what would we *do* with such a force? This question involves *doctrine,* and nuclear doctrine has two aspects: (1) What do we aim at? This is *targeting.* (2) Who strikes first? I call this *precedence of use.*

These aspects of doctrine lead inevitably to considerations of morality. It can't be avoided: morality and strategic doctrine are intertwined. They would be inextricable at the moment some future President had to make a decision to *use* the nuclear forces at his disposal. In the extremity of choice, leaders wouldn't simply

34

go ahead with their preplanned options and their doomsday responses. And because they wouldn't *simply* do that (though they might conceivably end up doing it), whole strategies, force structures, and doctrines might, in an instant of reflection, be negated by a flicker of moral concern (or moral cowardice, as some might have it). So we might as well take morality into consideration at the *beginning* of the process of considering nuclear strategies, since it would be pertinent at the moment of execution.

A nuclear strategy deliberately designed to be moral would start with two main concerns: (1) to avoid, as far as possible, civilian deaths in a nuclear war; and (2) to minimize the possibility of ever using nuclear weapons.

The trouble with the nuclear doctrines that have been adopted or asserted so far, the doctrines of countervalue and counterforce, is that they do not reconcile these two moral concerns. Measures that purport to limit damage to populations (i.e., counterforce) have entailed the kinds of weapons systems (combining accuracy with high yields, selective control, and large numbers of warheads) that destabilize the nuclear balance and so increase the likelihood of the use of nuclear weapons in a war. Measures to reduce the likelihood of nuclear war have up to now consisted primarily of increasing the contingent probability and horror of retaliation against civilians (i.e., countervalue), and this effect has been reinforced by the fact that the weapons systems expected to survive a preemptive attack (air-delivered and submarine-launched bombs and missiles) are also those that, because of their inaccuracy, have been relatively restricted to civilian targets. (Some advocates of countervalue, who want its stability without its immorality, say it is permissible to threaten to do something one might not actually have to do. But they have no right to assume, in order to absolve themselves of serious moral choice, that perfect deterrence will always prevail.)

It is possible with nuclear doctrine, just as it was with nuclear posture, to find another way, one that reconciles the two profound moral principles of sparing noncombatants and avoiding war. As some have pointed out, avoiding civilian deaths in a nuclear war calls for a "countercombatant" targeting doctrine, or

35

the targeting of the aggressor nation's military forces. This need *not* be counterforce in the sense, say, of James Schlesinger's "retargeting doctrine" of January 1974, or of Robert McNamara's "Ann Arbor doctrine" of June 1962. To implement this targeting doctrine, U.S. forces would have to be tightly commanded and controlled, and accurate. Accuracy in itself is not evil. As long as we enhance the accuracy of weapons systems that are invulnerable, there is still no incentive for an adversary to initiate a first strike against them. Therefore, their accuracy is a neutral factor in its effect on strategic stability.

The second moral requisite, minimizing the possibility of ever using nuclear weapons, breaks into two components. The first is indirect: eliminating an *adversary's* incentive to attack our missiles, touching off our second strike. This can be achieved by adopting the posture suggested before, the scrapping of our "sitting-duck" land-based missiles. The second component is more direct: imposing restraints on *ourselves* to prevent us from launching a first strike on the adversary's nuclear forces. There was a time when implementing the first objective, giving up land-based missiles, would have automatically accomplished the second, because sea-based missiles were so inaccurate that they could not be relied on to hit an enemy's missiles. Consequently there would have been no sound reason for us to fire them first. But as accurate guidance is built into our submarine-launched missiles (global satellite positioning and terminal homing systems), they become reliable for use in a preemptive strike.

So this leads to the second component of minimizing nuclear war, and the last component of this "modest proposal": Since we cannot any longer solve the moral problem of avoiding nuclear war just by making a quick fix in our posture, we must face squarely the question of the doctrine of precedence of use. We must impose upon ourselves a stringent *no-first-use* doctrine: We would not use nuclear weapons except in response to a nuclear attack on our own territory; and even then, we would strike only at military targets, even if the adversary's attack had hit our cities.

Others have proposed a no-first-use doctrine (for example, Richard H. Ullman in "No First Use of Nuclear Weapons,"

36

Foreign Affairs, July 1972, and Bruce M. Russett in "No First Use of Nuclear Weapons," *Worldview,* November 1976). But no one has joined it with such restrictive conditions for our retaliatory strike. Of course, if American cities were damaged by an enemy's nuclear attack, it would be nearly impossible, politically and psychologically, for a President to restrict our counterattack to military targets. Yet even then there is a valid argument, both practical and moral, for such restraint. Striking "enemy" populations would divert our nuclear weapons from more significant military targets. It would make no more strategic sense than it ever did, and no moral sense at all.

Choices

A nuclear policy based on a dyad of forces and a doctrine of no-cities and no-first-use does not solve all problems. But neither has any other nuclear policy, past or present, actual or hypothetical. In designing a nuclear policy, we are confronted with three possible flaws: instability, immorality, or incredibility. We can avoid as many as two of these flaws, but we can't avoid them all, entirely.

The policy proposed here would impair the credibility of our "extended deterrence," that is, the protective nuclear umbrella that we now purport to hold over our allies. Since our nuclear riposte would be strictly reserved as a response to a nuclear attack on our own territory, and our retaliation would be limited to military targets, the "coupling" of our strategic nuclear arsenal and our alliance commitments would be cut. In turn, the attempt to restrain nuclear proliferation might be hampered.

But, from everything we have seen in the past twenty years, our nuclear coupling is already somewhat less than whole. The days of John Foster Dulles and cheap extended deterrence are gone forever. In fact, our alliance commitments have long ago been eroded, implicitly and inevitably, by the advent of nuclear competition itself. In an era of nuclear parity and "nuclear plenty," the probability that a protector state would have the will to use its ultimate weapon to defend an ally might still be sufficient to deter a potential aggressor; but it is not always sufficient to convince the ally itself.

These "new facts" of nuclear trust and terror do not in themselves dictate the abandonment of our alliances. No one likes to disturb the shape of our associations, or deflect sympathy from the polities, societies, and civilizations of Western Europe, Israel, and Japan. But assurances of loyalty unfortunately don't have strategic value; they don't impress our allies much, either. The real question is not the shape but the implicit *content* of our alliances; not what we would like to do, but what we are *likely* to do, in the face of certain challenges. This is what has been changing, as our strategic circumstances change. And this is what concerns our allies.

In short, there are already holes in our nuclear umbrella, though optimists would not care to notice them until we had to open it. What can be done to compensate for an increasingly ambiguous nuclear commitment? This is not an essay on the repair of alliances, but it is fair to note that there are only two basic answers. Some people conclude that we should—and can—muster the national will to strengthen the common conventional defense, particularly in Europe. Others suspect that we ourselves cannot elicit the larger resources needed to offset a Soviet conventional buildup in the center and on the flanks of NATO, and conclude that we should "devolve" the additional defensive responsibilities to our allies. Though they also now lack the political will, we might at least hope that their situation, and our abstention, would force greater efforts toward their own defense.

But before we arrive at this exacting choice, there are two considerations that might provide some relief, if we grasp their implications and their opportunities. One is the fact that we could make a dozen improvements in our conventional posture in Europe that would cost little and in some cases nothing—improvements in the command of forces, the standardization and "interoperability" of weapons systems, the integration of logistics and communications, the redeployment of units, etc. The other consideration is that, in conventional just as in nuclear confrontation, an adversary will hesitate in the face of far less perfect deterrence than might be comfortable for an ally.

In any case, we should not, as we do now, depend residually and mindlessly on the first or indiscriminate use of nuclear weapons to defend our alliances, to take up the slack in our defensive preparations and bridge the strategic contradictions of our present policies. In making hard choices among less than satisfying alternatives, we must not convert a dilemma of regional conventional defense into a prescription for global nuclear holocaust.

To the ultimate questions of deterrence and alliance there are no uncomplicated answers. But at this juncture of strategic choice, there is a direction we can take that is constructive. Will our government pursue this direction—strategic restraint—not as a bargaining ploy but as a path to stability?

Surveying the swaying scaffolding of deténte, many of those who hope for peace are saying that the first objective is to restore political confidence and good will with the Soviets—that technical arrangements will follow. This is not necessarily so. Trust must be founded on the technical and logical conditions of strategic stability. Just as lack of trust can impede efforts to control arms, strategic instability can raise suspicions and undermine political confidence and good will.

If we are going to succeed in either objective—restoring trust or restoring stability—we will have to pursue both.

RECOMMENDED READING

Aaron, David. "SALT: A New Concept." *Foreign Policy* 17 (Winter 1974–75): 157–65.

Alperovitz, Gar. *Cold War Essays*. Cambridge, Mass.: Schenkman, 1970.

Ambrose, Stephen E. *Rise to Globalism: American Foreign Policy, 1938–1976*. New York: Penguin, 1976.

Aspin, Les. "How to Look at the Soviet-American Balance." *Foreign Policy* 22 (Spring 1976): 96–106.

Barnaby, Frank. "The Mounting Prospects of Nuclear War." *Bulletin of the Atomic Scientists,* June 1977, pp. 11–20.

————, et al., eds. *Arms Uncontrolled* (Stockholm International Peace Research Institute), p. 232. Cambridge: Harvard University Press, 1975.

Barnes, Harry Elmer. "A. J. P. Taylor and the Causes of World War II." *New Individualist Review* 2 (Spring 1962): 3–16.

————. *Perpetual War for Perpetual Peace*. Caldwell, Idaho: Caxton, 1953.

Barnet, Richard. "Promise of Disarmament." *New York Times Magazine,* 27 February 1977, p. 16.

————. *Roots of War*. New York: Penguin, 1973.

Bartlett, Bruce. "In Defense of Isolationism." *Libertarian Review,* March 1978, pp. 30–34.

Beard, Charles A. *President Roosevelt and the Coming of the War, 1941.* New Haven: Yale University Press, 1948.

———, and Smith, G. H. E. *The Idea of National Interest: An Analytical Study in American Foreign Policy.* New York: Macmillan, 1934.

Bernstein, Barton J. "The Cuban Missile Crisis." In *Reflections on the Cold War: A Quarter Century of American Foreign Policy,* edited by Lynn H. Miller and Ronald W. Pruessen, pp. 108–42. Philadelphia, Temple University Press, 1974.

———. "SALT: The Dangerous Illusion." *Inquiry,* 24 July 1978, pp. 16–19.

———, ed. *The Atomic Bomb: The Critical Issues.* Boston: Little, Brown, 1976.

———, ed. *Politics and Policies of the Truman Administration.* New York: Watts, 1970.

Bohn, Lewis C. "Is Nuclear Deterrence Really Necessary?" *War/Peace Report* 12 (1972): 3–9.

Boston Study Group. *The Price of Defense: A New Strategy for Military Spending.* New York: Times Books, 1978.

Bresler, Robert J. *The Ideology of the Executive State.* Menlo Park, Calif.: Institute for Humane Studies, 1973

Carter, Barry E. "Nuclear Strategy and Nuclear Weapons." *Scientific American,* May 1974, pp. 20–31.

Chamberlin, William H. *America's Second Crusade.* Colorado Springs, Colo.: Ralph Myles, 1962.

Cohen, Stephen F. "Why Détente Can Work." *Inquiry,* 19 December 1977, pp. 11–17.

Doenecke, Justus D. *The Literature of Isolationism: A Guide to Noninterventionist Scholarship, 1930–1972.* Colorado Springs, Colo.: Ralph Myles, 1972.

———. *Not to the Swift: The "Old" Isolationists in the Cold War Era.* Lewisburg, Pa.: Bucknell University Press, 1979.

———. "Review Essay: The Isolationists and a Usable Past." *Peace and Change* 5 (Spring 1978): 67–74.

Ekirch, Arthur A., Jr. *The Decline of American Liberalism.* New York: Atheneum, 1969.

———. *The Civilian and the Military: A History of the American Anti-military Tradition.* Colorado Springs, Colo.: Ralph Myles, 1972.

Epstein, William. *The Last Chance: Nuclear Proliferation and Arms Control.* New York: Free Press, 1976.

Etzold, Thomas H. *Why America Fought Germany in World War II.* St. Louis, Mo.· Forum Press, 1973.

Fairgate, Alan. "Non-Marxist Theories of Imperialism." *Reason,* February 1976, pp. 46–52.

Fleming, D. F. *The Cold War and Its Origins, 1917–1960.* New York: Doubleday, 1961.

Flynn, John T. *As We Go Marching.* New York: Free Life, 1973.

Gaddis, John L. *The United States and the Origins of the Cold War, 1941–1947.* New York: Columbia University Press, 1972.

Gardner, Lloyd C. *Architects of Illusion: Men and Ideas in American Foreign Policy, 1941–1949.* New York: Watts, 1972.

Gray, Colin S. *The Soviet-American Arms Race.* Lexington, Mass.: Lexington Books, 1976.

———. "Détente, Arms Control and Strategies: Perspectives on SALT." *American Political Science Review* 70 (December 1976): 1242–56.

Jonas, Manfred. *Isolationism in America, 1935–1941.* Ithaca, N.Y.: Cornell University Press, 1969.

Jordan, Amos A., et al. "Soviet Strength, U.S. Purpose." *Foreign Policy* 23 (Summer 1976): 32–52.

Kahan, Jerome. *Security in the Nuclear Age: Developing U.S. Strategic Arms Policy.* Washington, D.C.: Brookings Institution, 1975.

Kaplan, Fred. "NATO and the Soviet Scare." *Inquiry,* 22 June 1978, pp. 16–20.

Kennan, George F. "The United States and the Soviet Union, 1917–1976." *Foreign Affairs* 54 (July 1976): 670–90.

———. *The Cloud of Danger: Current Realities of American Foreign Policy.* Boston: Little, Brown, 1977.

Kirkendall, Richard S. *The Truman Period as a Research Field: A Reappraisal, 1972.* Columbia: University of Missouri, 1973.

Kolko, Gabriel. *The Roots of American Foreign Policy: An Analysis of Power and Purpose.* Boston: Beacon, 1969.

———. *The Politics of War: The World and United States Foreign Policy, 1943–1945.* New York: Random House, 1968.

———, and Kolko, Joyce. *The Limits of Power: The World and United States Foreign Policy, 1945-1954.* New York: Harper & Row, 1972.

LaFeber, Walter. *America, Russia and the Cold War, 1945-1975.* New York: Wiley, 1976.

———, ed. *America in the Cold War: Twenty Years of Revolution and Response, 1947-1967.* New York: Wiley, 1969.

Lambeth, Benjamin S. "The Evolving Soviet Strategic Threat." *Current History* 69 (October 1975): 121-25.

Lens, Sidney. *The Futile Crusade: Anti-Communism as American Credo.* Chicago: Quadrangle, 1964.

Liggio, Leonard P. *Why the Futile Crusade?* New York: Center for Libertarian Studies, 1978.

———. "Cold War Revisionism: The Major Historical Task." *Left and Right* 2 (Spring 1966): 17-30.

———, and Martin, James J., eds. *Watershed of Empire: Essays on New Deal Foreign Policy.* Colorado Springs, Colo.: Ralph Myles, 1976.

Lodal, Jan M. "Assuring Strategic Stability: An Alternate View." *Foreign Affairs* 54 (April 1976): 462-81.

———. "Verifying SALT." *Foreign Policy* 24 (Fall 1976): 40-64.

Long, Franklin A., and Rathjens, George W., eds. *Arms, Defense Policy and Arms Control.* New York: Norton, 1976.

Macdonagh, Oliver. "The Anti-Imperialism of Free Trade." *Economic History Review* 14 (April 1962): 489-501.

Martin, James J. *American Liberalism and World Politics.* Old Greenwich, Conn.: Devin-Adair, 1963.

———. *Revisionist Viewpoints: Essays in a Dissident Historical Tradition.* Colorado Springs, Colo.: Ralph Myles, 1971.

Melman, Seymour. *Pentagon Capitalism: The Political Economy of War.* New York: McGraw-Hill, 1970.

———. *The Permanent War Economy: American Capitalism in Decline.* New York: Simon & Schuster, 1974.

Mills, C. Wright. *Causes of World War Three.* Westport, Conn.: Greenwood Press, 1976.

Mises, Ludwig von. *Liberalism: A Socioeconomic Exposition.* Kansas City: Sheed Andrews & McMeel, 1978.

Moon, Parker T. *Imperialism and World Politics.* New York: Macmillan, 1927.

Morley, Felix. *The Foreign Policy of the United States.* New York: Knopf, 1951.

———. "American Republic or American Empire." *Modern Age* 1 (Summer 1957): 20–32.

Myrdal, Alva. *The Game of Disarmament: How the United States and Russia Run the Arms Race.* New York: Pantheon, 1976.

Neumann, William L. *America Encounters Japan: From Perry to MacArthur.* Baltimore: Johns Hopkins Press, 1963.

Patterson, Thomas G., ed. *Cold War Critics.* Chicago: Quadrangle, 1971.

Pierre, Andrew J., and Moyne, Claudia W. *Nuclear Proliferation: A Strategy for Control.* Headline Series, no. 232. New York: Foreign Policy Association, 1976.

Polmar, Norman. *Strategic Weapons: An Introduction.* New York: Crane, Russak, 1975.

Radosh, Ronald. *Prophets on the Right: Conservative Critics of American Globalism.* New York: Simon & Schuster, 1975.

Ravenal, Earl C. *Never Again: Learning from America's Foreign Policy Failures.* Philadelphia: Temple University Press, 1978.

———. *Toward World Security: A Program for Disarmament.* Washington, D.C.: Institute for Policy Studies, 1978.

———. *NATO's Unremarked Demise.* Berkeley: University of California Institute of International Studies, 1979.

———. "Foreign Policy Consensus: Who Needs It?" *Foreign Policy* 18 (Spring 1975): 80–91.

———. "Consequences of the End Game in Vietnam." *Foreign Affairs* 53 (July 1975): 651–67.

———. "An Autopsy of Collective Security." *Political Science Quarterly* 90 (Winter 1975–76): 697–714.

———. "After Schlesinger: Something Has to Give." *Foreign Policy* 22 (Spring 1976):71–95.

———. "Non-Intervention: A Libertarian Approach to Defense." *Reason,* July 1977, pp. 16–20.

———. "The Way Out of Korea." *Inquiry,* 5 December 1977, pp. 15–18.

———. "How to Cut the Defense Budget." *Inquiry,* 1 May 1978, pp. 18–21.

———. "Does Disarmament Have a Future?" *Nation,* 27 May 1978, pp. 636–40.

———. "The Middle East After Camp David: Walking on Water." *Libertarian Review,* October 1978, pp. 17–25.

———, and Chace, James, eds. *Atlantis Lost: U.S.-European Relations After the Cold War.* New York: New York University Press, 1976.

Rosecrance, Richard N. "Détente or Entente?" *Foreign Affairs* 53 (April 1975): 464–81.

Rothbard, Murray N. *For a New Liberty: The Libertarian Manifesto,* pp. 263–96. New York: Macmillan, 1978.

———. "War, Peace, and the State." *Standard,* April 1963, p. 2.

Rubinstein, Alvin Z. "Soviet-American Relations." *Current History* 71 (October 1976): 101.

Russett, Bruce M. *No Clear and Present Danger: A Skeptical View of the United States Entry into World War II.* New York: Harper & Row, 1972.

Shulman, Marshall D. "On Learning to Live with Authoritarian Regimes." *Foreign Affairs* 55 (January 1977): 325–38.

Stone, I. F. *The Hidden History of the Korean War.* New York: Monthly Review, rev. ed. 1969.

Sumner, William Graham. *The Conquest of the United States by Spain, and Other Essays.* Chicago: Regnery, 1965.

Swomley, John. *American Empire: The Political Ethics of 20th Century Conquest.* New York: Macmillan, 1972.

Taft, Robert. *A Foreign Policy for Americans.* Garden City, N.Y.: Doubleday, 1951.

Tansill, Charles C. *America Goes to War* (1938). Reprint. Gloucester, Mass.: Peter Smith, 1963.

———. *Back Door to War: The Roosevelt Foreign Policy, 1933–1941.* Chicago: Regnery, 1952.

Theoharis, Athan. "The Origins of the Cold War: A Revisionist Interpretation." *Peace and Change* 4 (Fall 1976): 3–11.

Tucker, Robert W. *A New Isolationism: Threat or Promise?* Washington, D.C.: Potomac Association, 1972.

Veale, F. J. P. *Advance to Barbarism: A Reexamination.* Old Greenwich, Conn.: Devin-Adair, 1968.

Walton, Richard J. *Cold War and Counterrevolution: The Foreign Policy of John F. Kennedy,* pp. 103–42 (chap. 7, "The Cuban Missile Crisis"). New York: Viking, 1972.

Warnke, Paul C. "Apes on a Treadmill." *Foreign Policy* 18 (Spring 1975): 12–29.

Williams, William A. *The Tragedy of American Diplomacy.* New York: Dell, 1972.

———. *The Contours of American History.* Cleveland: World, 1961.

Yannov, Alex. *Détente After Brezhnev.* Berkeley: University of California Institute of International Studies, 1977.

York, Herbert C. *Race to Oblivion.* New York: Simon & Schuster, 1970.

NOTE: I would like to thank David J. Theroux for compiling this valuable bibliography. —ECR

ABOUT THE AUTHOR

Earl C. Ravenal received his B.A. from Harvard University, and his M.A. and Ph.D. from Johns Hopkins University. He was Director of the Asian Division in the Office of the Secretary of Defense from 1967 to 1969. He is now a professor of international relations at the Georgetown School of Foreign Service and a Fellow of the Institute for Policy Studies.

Dr. Ravenal is co-author and editor of *Peace with China? U.S. Decisions for Asia;* co-author and co-editor of *Atlantis Lost: U.S.-European Relations after the Cold War;* and author of *Never Again: Learning from America's Foreign Policy Failures, Foreign Policy in an Uncontrollable World* (forthcoming), and *NATO's Unremarked Demise.*

His contributions appear in the following volumes, among others: *Armed Conflict in the 1980s* (ed. R. H. Ullman); *The Lessons of Vietnam* (ed. W. S. Thompson and D. D. Frizzell); *The Legacy of Vietnam: The War, American Society, and the Future of American Foreign Policy* (ed. A. K. Lake); *Problems of the Federal Budget* (ed. M. G. Raskin); *The United States in World Affairs: Leadership, Partnership, or Disengagement?* (ed. R. A. Bauer).

Dr. Ravenal's articles and reviews have appeared in numerous journals, including *Foreign Affairs; Foreign Policy; American Political Science Review; Asian Survey; The Atlantic; Defense Monitor; Foreign Service Journal; Inquiry; Libertarian Review; New Republic; Asia-Pacific Community; Political Science Quarterly; Policy Studies Journal; The Nation.*